For Audrey Margarita Kellett

I0487232

A Scoping Study into the Perceptions of Phonological Pedagogy in Rural Ghana

Christopher John Counihan

First published, 2009
United Kingdom
Lulu Publishing Ltd

ISBN: 978-1-4452-1756-7

Cover Design by Lulu Cover Wizard
Printed By Lulu Print

"A tree that doesn't know how to dance, will be taught by the wind"

Ghanaian Proverb

Abstract

C hildren's linguistic development is under threat in Ghana. English is the national language, however with a multi-lingual demographic; children are not receiving adequate training in both their native and second languages. The recent educational reforms have placed an emphasis on implementing early year's education into the Ghanaian curriculum. Under these new measures children will receive free nursery and kindergarten education. Whilst this is a significant step forward in re-shaping educational provision, language development in both native and second languages is severely underdeveloped. After three years of kindergarten education, children enter the first year of primary school illiterate. The primary curriculum expects the children to read textbooks in English at this level. Furthermore, the unstructured nature of English teaching isn't made compulsory until the higher primary years. Therefore, the language of instruction at this level is predominately mixed with both English and the mother tongue.

This scoping study aims at seeking the opinions of professionals to whether a phonics programme can be potentially implemented into the early year's curriculum. The analysis of this research was supplemented by interviews and questionnaires with educational professionals from the KEEA district in rural Ghana. In considering the results and the empirical insights found in the interviews and questionnaires, an emphasis on a structured culturally sustainable phonics programme is recognised as the method of tackling illiteracy in the early years and improving children's linguistic development.

Acknowledgments

I would personally like to thank my fiancée Lisa Marie Simnett for assisting with this book from the original research to the proof reading and editing of the final piece. Without your sound judgement, critical analysis and general support, the focus of this book would have resulted in failure.

The Sabre Charitable Trust team have shown a clear design and foundation of how curricula frameworks can be managed and sustained successfully. Through their vision of opportunity, children and their families are benefiting greatly in areas of deprivation than ever before. Therefore, I would like to personally thank Dominic Bond, Aubrey Malcolm Green and Tom Malcolm Green for their professional support and guidance during the research period of this publication.

This book is dedicated to all the children of KEEA and professionals that serve them on a day to day basis. Without your insight and direction, our partnership for change would be in jeopardy.

List of Acronyms

CRIQPEG - Centre for Research in Primary Education Quality

ECCE - Early Childhood Care and Education

FCUBE - Free Compulsory Basic Education Programme

GES- Ghana Education Service

GPHC - Ghana Population Housing Census

GOG - Government of Ghana

JHS - Junior High School

KEEA - Komenda-Edina-Eguafo-Abrem

KG - Kindergarten

LAD - Language Acquisition Device

MOESS - Ministry of Education Science and Sport

NGO - Non Government Organisation

SCT - Sabre Charitable Trust

SSS - Senior Secondary School

Chapter I

Introduction

1.1Aims of the Research

This study is a formative evaluation piece of research into the perceptions of whether phonological strategies can be implemented into a primary school's literacy curriculum in rural Ghana. The study was based primarily on three semi-structured interviews of key professionals working in the Komenda-Edina-Eguafo-Abrem (KEEA) district of Ghana. Each of the participants has a professional relationship with the school and the development of its curriculum. To assist the findings, eight other primary schools within the region were selected by random to participate in a structured questionnaire.

1.2 Structure of Study

The first chapter begins with the introductory information that surrounds this study. It will give an insight to the factors of why this scoping study into phonologic pedagogy, has the potential of improving literacy in the early years.

Chapter 2 of the study is the literary overview of theories, frameworks and educational systems. Given the complexities involved with providing one overview of the literature, this section is divided into three sub-sections:

- The first section recognises the theorising of language development from prior research. It provides the foundation of how children establish language and the developmental factors that relate to the empirical and theoretical findings.

- The second section concerns itself with the phonics debate from a British context. It draws upon the arguments made in the past and chronologically traces the steps towards the practices used today in British classrooms.

- The last section addresses the Ghanaian education system with the emphasis on literacy development. This section investigates the steps taken towards literacy education and communicates the struggles going forward.

The remainder of this report, starting from chapter three, consists of the research itself. From the beginning of this chapter, the study takes shape by detailing the methodologies used in acquiring the data. Chapter four produces the presentation of results from the interviews and questionnaires. A detailed analysis of the data and comparisons are made with regard to the holistic research. This section will then be further analysed with relation to the empirical and theoretical findings from the literature. The discussion chapter will also document these findings with regard to the main points raised from the findings. Finally, chapter six details the conclusions of the study with the emphasis placed upon recommendations and future study.

1.3 Background to Why Study is Needed

In Ghana, most children will enter nursery or school speaking very little or no English (Arnett, 2007, p350). English is the national language of the country, but it is seen as a second language throughout the whole country (Dakabu, 1988). Since Ghana's independence from the United Kingdom in 1957, English has emerged from politics as the instructional language of the country. However, other indigenous and regional dialects have greater significance in social situations (Agawu, 2003, p39). Language demographic structure has no common similarity within Ghana's districts, with some 44 indigenous languages and dialects being spoken (Obeng & Hartford, 2002, p135). Therefore, the regional aspect of these languages makes it difficult to establish a holistic national English literacy programme. The teaching of English is confined to small affluent areas of the country, which makes limited accessibility for all socio-sub groups (Naylor, 2000). In general terms, education is seen as a luxury that is administered only to wealthy Ghanaians who can afford it (Fennell & Arnot, 2007). Furthermore, children who can access education are expected to learn both their native language merged with English programmes. There is significant empirical research to suggest that by combining native tongue teachings with English as a second language, children are failing to grasp the basic skills of either (see Obeng & Hartford, 2002, Newell, 2002). The Ghanaian education system identifies English within its curriculum. However, this is severely underdeveloped in the early years as teaching is merged with both mother tongue and English (MOE, 1999). In cognitive and language acquisition terms, this instruction, with relation to outputs, signals a mixed message rather than a concomitant alignment.

Since September 2007 a synthetic phonics approach to the teaching of reading, writing and other aspects of social and emotional development is helping children in the UK to read and write at higher rates than previous years (Ward, 2009). The following research discusses this topic further and develops whether this success can be implemented internationally and whether the same techniques can be applied into an already demanding curriculum.

1.4 Sabre Charitable Trust

An English charity that works for educational improvement in Ghana has reported that because of a lack of structure, children are moving from kindergarten to primary school illiterate (*Teaching Methodology- Sabretrust.org*).

The Sabre Charitable Trust (SCT) is a small NGO that works with three schools in Ghana, to help improve literacy and whole educational issues. The trust has put in place an ethical volunteering programme that enlists professionals and students to embark on providing an educational experience into the schools. Preliminary findings from volunteer placements suggest that a structured culturally sustainable phonics programme would be best suited in the schools and that it would help improve literacy attainment. Therefore, the main aim of this research is to understand whether this can be achieved, and whether a programme can be implemented in accordance with the local government and affiliated agencies. Accompanying this motivation is the desire to research the opinions of professionals that work with literacy agendas, and to gauge their thoughts on the potential development of phonologic practice.

The study also holds personal interest with the researcher as a practical piece of action research. It is hoped that the findings in this study will back-up the movements made by the charity in improving educational outcomes for children in early year's education in KEEA.

1.6 Research Questions

With the direct interest surrounding this research, the following two questions were formed to formulate a plan to help answer the research problem:

- What are the perceptions of a phonics strategy to assist the teaching of English in a rural village in Ghana?
- Which type of phonics approach, whether analytic or synthetic, is seen as the best method of pedagogy in the KEEA district?

Chapter II

Review of the Literature

Introduction

A large body of the literature from psycholinguistic, educationalists and international perspectives provides the basis for the present study. This chapter will explain the process of studies included from the development of language acquisition to educational perspectives here in the UK and Ghana. The broad search of literature that features within this chapter examines both the theoretical and empirical studies that concern this topic.

2.1 Language Design

The nature of how children acquire language and construct lexicon has been part of the revolutionary cognitive psychology movement and argument for the past 40 years (Davis, 2007). Since Chomsky and Halle's book, *The Sound Pattern of English* (1968) and their early work on transformational phonology, many pioneers like Patricia Kuhl, Jacques Mehler, Janet Werker, Peter Eiames and Peter Jusczyk have placed the nature of language acquisition as the flagship of their inquiry and of developmental psychology (Pepekamp, 2003). The consensual view around phonological approaches to language acquisition is that there is a common core of knowledge across all languages (Goldsmith, 1999). Chomsky and Halle (1968) argue that children have innate knowledge of generative proportions that can be contrasted further in language development (Chomsky & Halle, 1968). Chomsky himself proclaimed,

"As far as we know, possession of human language is associated with a specific type of mental organisation, not simply a higher degree of intelligence". (Chomsky, p70, 1970).

Essentially, Chomsky proposed that through his language acquisition device (LAD) children generated complex syntactic structures way before them starting any formal education (Hall and Marsh, 2003). With the views of Chomsky's LAD paradigm, Pinker (1994) developed the argument further by theorising that language acquisition is broadly based around four themes (cited in Oates & Grayson, 2004). Pinker's themes were around the science of brain function and the re-creation of language moving from minor *"pidgins"* to *"spoken creoles"* with the inclusion of a *"poverty of input"* and *"universal grammar"* (Pinker, 1994, p12). Ultimately, Pinker's work endorsed an innate protocol which suggests that language is universal as children re-invent it following a set of grammatical rules (Pinker,1994). Goldin-Meadow & Feldman (1977) back up this claim by providing biological evidence with a study of four congenitally deaf children who had not been exposed to sign language (cited in Gross, 1999). The children constructed their own signs which showed a preliminary call of communicative rule. Upon reflection, this relates to Pinker's philosophy, as the children formed a way of communicating, which suggests the possibility of an innate need to understand and construct language whether it is spoken or signed. However, Pinker did support a claim that without rules there cannot be a universal understanding of language, he states:

"The ubiquity of complex language among human beings is a gripping discovery and, for many observers, compelling proof that language is innate. But to tough minded sceptics it is no proof at all. Not everything that is universal is innate". (Pinker, 1994, p 31).

Upon reflection of Pinker's ideas, it is important to see that language may indeed follow an innate path. However, the same path cannot be followed by all. This representation builds around the different ways we communicate and that language construction follows an evolutionary schema. Additionally, the work of Jerry Fodor's modular processing unit in the brain, which works outside of human consciousness, identifies language as something we cannot control with particular reference to the difference between hearing and listening (cited in Carrol, 2001). The vast amount of literature suggests a concomitant agreement of the research around the innate application of language. With the likes of Chomsky, Fodor and Pinker leading the inquiry, their work is often categorised in the literature as advocators of the Chomskyian Innateisim Movement (see Chomsky & Otero, 2004, Hanna, 2006, Field, 2007).

Conversely, many linguistics and language anthropologists argued that Chomsky's Innateism approach does not adequately address the social dimensions and experiences of other communicative methods (see Labov, 1972, Hymes, 1972, Rogoff, 2003,). Such views, including that of Jean Piaget, spoke of how language differs as it follows a complex structure that builds upon interactions between children's current linguistic and non linguistic environments (Bohannon, 1993). This view is often represented as a Piagetian Constructivism (see Piattelli-Palmarini,1980; Talay-Ongan & Ap, 2005). Piaget disagreed on many levels of Chomsky's work especially around the semantics in language design (Cattell, 2004). Semantics, in linguistic production relates to the expressed meaning of words (Shaffer, 1993). Therefore, children will recognise words and understand that there is meaning associated with each new word they learn. From this, children will use visual reasoning to accompany verbal alignment. Piaget believed that the semantic design in language grew with the child and that the thoughts and actions were represented through semantic conceptuality, built from the environment (Owens, 1988). In the beginning this may be represented by a child who uses words, but not in a syntactical manner. The research of De Villiers & De Villers (1978) best describes this process at the pre-linguistic stage of development. They explain that babies often produced every known phoneme that occurs in the human language. These early noises provide the preliminary foundations of what will build towards single word and grammar association. The literature consults this work as identifiably born from a behaviourist's view around reinforcement and imitation from the parent, which was originally identified by B. F. Skinner (cited in Maitland & Hannah, 2007). To summarise, this view is heavily based around environmental factors when constructing lexicon and furthering language development.

Upon reflection, the literature considers both innate and constructive movements as an integral part of the future of understanding language acquisition. Where the battle of language was initially around fabrication, the cognitive psychology movement holistically advocated phonology as a discipline through strategies that includes acoustic, suprasegmental and segmental methods of acquisition (Strauss, 2005, Anderson & Ewen, 1987). The literature suggests that there is enough empirical evidence that is closely linked with Piaget's sensor-motor stage development. However, the innate factors draw interesting questions. How do we know language is not entirely learned or imitated? Given the many factors of language construction, how can a child learn so fast without any pre-wiring? Alternatively, can there be a co-existence of both theories that supplements the engineering process of language? The literature doesn't answer these questions directly, but weaves in arguments that have featured extensively in this review. To evaluate, there is no axiomatic truth relating to both arguments, but single approaches that seem to search for claims. Pepekamp (2003) summarises both arguments around the fact that children have a universal language outlook, but further research around how they acquire it needs to be developed.

2.2 Analytic Versus Synthetic

With the acceptance of phonology as a key component of language acquisition (whether through innate or constructivist approaches), the need to develop strategy to accommodate learning has also been a widely contested issue in the United Kingdom's Literacy Frameworks (see Goodman *et al*, 2003, Mallet, 2008). Holistically, phonics much like other teaching strategies has been thrown into and out of favour since the beginning out the 18th Century (Cove, 2006). Cove (2006) evaluates the historical content and mentions that unhelpful phonic dichotomy over the years has resulted in pedagogical struggle. She continued by stating:

"The most contested issues - of what form phonics approach to use, how systematic it should be, when to start it, how fast to pace it, run through the history as familiar leitmotivs" (Cove, 2006, p111).

Phonological strategies have unequivocally contributed to the teaching of reading and literacy in general. Best practice seems to revel around the strategy itself rather than identifying the importance of supporting the teacher who will have to deliver a programme. This has been pointed out on numerous occasions over the years with particular regard to the countless research and national agenda publications (Diack, 1965, Southgate & Roberts, 1970). The Bullock Report (1975), *A Language for Life* concluded:

"There is no one method, medium, approach, device, or philosophy that holds the key to learning to read" (DES, 1975, p521).

For the majority of the 1980's and early 1990's, phonological methods were largely down to the analytic approach for delivery. The reclassification of the scientific terminology was largely down to the methods mentioned in Bielby's (1994) *Making Sense of Reading*. Not only did this book make significant discoveries in the process of advancing phonic pedagogy, it birthed the analytic approach, and thus the phonic wars began.

Analytic phonics can be seen in practical terms as the way children segment a particular whole word, whereas individual phoneme sounds are commonly regarded as a synthetic approach to learning (Lewis & Ellis, 2006). More confusingly, the call for alternative methods, and in some cases a multi-integrated approach, was seen as "good practice" by the introduction of the National Literacy Strategy (NLS) *Framework for Teaching* publication (DfEE, 1998). This period was seen to be short lived as Johnson and Watson's study in Clackmannanshire found that children would benefit from a single operant synthetic phonics programme (SOEID, 1998). The research contained two studies conducted over a period of seven years looking at the synthetic and analytic approaches (Johnston & Watson, 2004). The literature consults the commentary around this study with few academics acknowledging its validity. According to Hall (2006), the design fabric of the research was flawed as there was a biased link to the synthetic approach. However, other research (see Chew, 1997, Stuart *et al* 1999, Macmillian, 2002) found similar findings to that of the Clackmannanshire study with the benefits of a systematic synthetic programme. With the polarisation of pedagogical literacy development, the focus was ultimately seen to be more about practice led initiatives. Children would still receive 15 minutes of phonics that was sandwiched into the literacy hour. With the divide around practice, it is not clear in the literature which programme, at the time, was seen as the more widely used. No such research or data around how many schools used which approach is evident.

The second publication of the NLS focused around practice and delivery which was found in the NLS *Literacy Training Pack* (DfEE, 1998b). The literature relates to the continuing professional development of teachers and those who are new to the profession. In response, *Progression in Phonics* (DfEE, 1999a) was published to highlight a systematic approach to practice delivery in the classroom. Following this, *Teaching of Phonics in Primary Schools* (Ofsted, 2001) highlighted the various techniques teachers needed to apply for successful delivery; once again the report highlighted the coalition of analytic and synthetic approaches.

In the light of government and public interest, two seminars culminated in 2001 with Ofsted, and two with the UK Reading Association (now the UK Literacy Association) addressing the need for focus on one particular programme (Cook, 2002). These seminars brought together a range of professionals. The NLS responded with *Playing with Sounds* (DfES, 2003a) which addressed the question of whether a mixed approach was indeed necessary and redevelopment of how to pace a particular programme were particularly addressed. Upon evaluation, the document presented interesting facts, as once again, the debate ignored practitioner's inquiries for better clarity around phonic pedagogy. Ofsted's first report of the first four operative years of the NLS praised certain areas of phonics. However, it called for a single strategic approach with the emphasis for more focused research (Brooks, 2003). With a plethora of news articles and government debate around the best strategy, the House of Commons Education and Skills Select Committee set up an inquiry:

"We took evidence from witnesses who argued that "phonics" programmes should have more prominence in the early teaching of reading (these programmes concentrate on establishing an early understanding of sound-letter correspondence). We took evidence from others who questioned the utility of enrichment of linguistic experience, as well as from those who support the current Government advice in the form of the Primary National Strategy. Many of those who contacted us during this inquiry argued objectively which method worked best, based on the available evidence, or, if the evidence was insufficient, to recommend steps that should be taken in order to reach a conclusion. (House of Commons Education Skills Committee, 2005: para.3).

Following a widespread outcry for a review into literacy, Jim Rose (former HMI Director of Inspection at Ofsted), was asked to *"examine current evidence about practises for teaching children to read to ensure that the strategy can continue to provide the most effective support for assuring children's progression in reading"* (DfES, 2005a). Furthermore, the DfES made clear that *"Phonics is already a central part of the approaches recommended by the Primary National Strategy"* (DfES, 2005a). Therefore, the wide literature research proclaimed that phonics was indeed on the agenda, but how to enforce it shall need further research.

The Rose Review was setup to investigate the teaching of phonics in England, which culminated with arguably, the most controversial document on the teaching of reading (Wyse, 2006). The final report was available from March 2006 and concluded *"synthetic phonics offers the vast majority of young children the best and most direct route to becoming skilled readers and writers"* (DfES, 2006:4). Important factors were born from the review that was reliant around the intricate details of practice. In particular, the review noted *"Nearly half of the schools visited did not give enough time to teaching children the crucial skill of blending (synthesizing) sounds together"* (DfES, 2006: 232). Blending is a major part of practice with its relationship of individual phonemes that builds towards word construction. For example, a consonant, vowel, consonant (CVC) word, e.g. C-A-T, will be blended normally after children have learnt individual letters (and their corresponding sounds) each day in the school week, through playful scenarios with the last day consumed to blending the new phonemes to produce words (Huxford, 2006). The literature refers to the advantage of segmenting which is catalogued by the work of Bissex (1980), Read (1986) and Gentry (1982). Their work centred upon children's propensity to identify new phonemes and construct the sounds into words. The literature evaluates and thus agrees with the claim in the Rose Review that this should be the centre piece around practice. Ultimately the review concluded:

"The case for systematic phonic work is overwhelming and much strengthened by a synthetic approach" (Rose, 2006: 20).

While the reaction to the Inquiry was balanced, some studies support the Rose research findings. A systematic review of the research literature on the use of phonics in the teaching of reading and spelling, which ran parallel with the Rose Review (Torgesen et al, 2006), found that evidence for synthetic formulation was no greater than the analytic approaches. Much of the literature concerns itself with the compelling link to the Clackmannanshire study and the findings of the Rose Review (Wyse, 2006). This produces interesting questions to why other methods were not originally consulted. Why was this seen as the answer to accompany successful reading pedagogy? Rosen (2006) also indicates the complete disregard for other research (see Torgersen, et al, 2006), placing the emphasis of the report in schools that had simultaneous programmes running and schools that advocated the synthetic approach. However, with schools needing a clearer focus around practice and policy, the Rose Review reacted by stating,

"Schools and settings cannot always wait for the results of long term research studies. They must take decisions based on as much firm evidence as is available" (DfES, 2006:31).

In summary, the review does highlight important factors as outlined in this review of the literature. Most importantly it addresses a need to focus the future around practice and pedagogical advancement. Recently, the synthetic approach has been winning teachers over, as results have greatly improved through lessons that dedicate at least 20 minutes a day to teaching English (Ward, 2009). However, given the historical perspectives and champions of analytic approaches, is this just another swing in the pendulum?

Upon reflection of the literature around the inquiries and decisions taken, there is a certain amount of déjà vu around the decisions made with relation to recent history. The literature discusses the continual need to rediscover practice and search for claims, whilst in practice the divide around strategies are played out in classrooms throughout the UK. It almost seems that there is a phonic panic outbreak every 5-10 years (Lewis & Ellis, 2006). There is particular scrutiny into the strategies used and whether the chosen strategy is too fast or correctly paced? (*ibid*). The shift from the searchlights model has been a staple of progression and should not be used again to re-address what has clearly been reciprocated from generation to generation. The focus upon social, creative and enriching exemplars should play a greater role for the future.

2.3 Ghanaian Context of Early Years Illiteracy

The Rose Review makes international links with countries where Literacy can be seen to improve curriculum initiatives (Wyse *et al*, 2007). Such value can have important factors with literacy development in Ghana. Ammon (2007) *et al* identifies opportunities by suggesting that Anglophone African countries with interest for literacy development can reap educational benefits and tackle illiteracy in general. However, Ghana like many other Western African countries has a multi-lingual demographic (Mansour, 1993). Historically, colonised African countries have struggled with the integration of multi-language development into societies (Kortmann & Schneider, 2004). In Ghana, this can be traced back to the genesis of formal education through Christian missionaries, between 1529 and 1925 (Obeng & Hartford, 2002). This period can be characterised by the usage of the occupying languages that included Portuguese, Danish, Dutch and English (Graham, 1971).

Ghana's education system is in a present state of transition through the new educational reforms (Nesin, *et al*, 2008). However, throughout the literature it is well established that poverty is derailing the policies that have been set over the past 15 years (see Canagarajah and Coulombe, 1997). Dreze & Kingdon (2001) and Filmer & Pritchett (1999) argue that education can provide a path out of impoverishment, providing the government address the accessibility options for every society. One of the latest reforms is the ECCE that amended the FCUBE programme which began in 1995 (MOESS, 2000). Its main aim is to provide free schooling in the early years to encourage enrolment *(ibid)*. Whilst school participation grew in early years and primary schools (Rolleston, 2009), the initial projections to improve attainment in English and other core subjects have not yet been met (Wan, 2008). In a recent study into school participation, MOESS found that for every 1000th child who enters KG, only 559 progress through the primary system, 159 drop out, while 283 children had to repeat various years (MOESS, 2006). There are significant research gaps into the reasons why children drop out of school and the path they choose to follow. From a preliminary cross analysis of the narrative, there is not one common theme that emerges as the single factor. Instead, there are several arguments that opine as possible reasons. Wan (2008) argues that trends set by prior governments have had everlasting damaging effects, particularly highlighting a neglect to improve English as a cause of why children don't attend. In addition, Dei (2004) points to the underdeveloped and undervalued spiritual and religious recognition in the curriculum. Another argument, as recognised by Sunal and Mutua (2007), demonstrates the unaffordable costs of higher education and questions the significance of programmes against societal needs. All points have a plausible disposition into the theories that might suggest non-attendance. Indeed, the prevailing factor from all the arguments indicates the main reasons for children not developing educationally. Whilst there is no direct link towards children's linguistic development, it can be conceived that without educational guidance, children won't be able to develop linguistically (GOG, 2004). There is empirical evidence supported by the findings from MOESS that children are failing to develop English at every level from early year's to senior education (MOESS, 1999). Research conducted by the University of Cape Coast and CRIQPEG show that children who enter the first year of primary school are illiterate (CRIQPEG, 1995). The latest data conducted via the GPHC announced that 53% of females and 37% of males above the age of 15 years were found to be illiterate (cited in Arnett, 2007). Furthermore, just 24% of both girls and boys were enrolled in JHS and SSS *(ibid)*.

In Ghana, children begin formal education aged between four and six (Little, 2007). All teachings are instructed through the mother tongue with English as a second language, however by primary 4 the roles are reversed as English becomes the instructional language (Wan, 2008). In the literature, there seems to be a difference of which language is the instructional method used for teaching between schools in rural and urban areas (see Huber, 1999). With Relation to English as the instructional language, urban cities will have an abundance of English literature represented through newspapers, television and books *(ibid)*. Whilst it isn't recognised in the literature and depending on the linguistic homogeneous of classes, English is predictably exposed to children way before any formal primary education. Salm & Falola (2002) places an emphasis on Kindergartens and private schooling introducing English frameworks as the instructional language. Upon evaluation, the evidence from the literature points to the fact that children seem to be better off linguistically in urban areas rather than rural. There seems to be no specific comparative studies between rural and urban linguistic attainment. However, it is recorded from the standardised testing in JHS that children stay in school longer and are more likely to achieve than that of those in rural areas (MOE, 1999).

The instructional language, whether local tongue or English, is premised in the curriculum as the foundation that can be transmitted into the developing second language (MOE, 2000). Given the facts mentioned above, with particular highlight to children arriving into schools at various ages and the children's educational ability at these ages; is learning another language alongside the native tongue achievable in unstructured circumstances? With so many Ghanaian children already struggling to learn in their native language, can these skills be correctly deployed into a second language? Whilst the findings, as stated earlier by Chomsky and Halle (1968), proposed through a set of universal grammar rules children can transfer linguistically, language must be exposed from an early age. Indeed, Piaget's thoughts of children being products of the environment (see Piattelli-Palmarini, 1980) seem to be placed as the obvious fact for why children in rural areas achieve less than those who learn in urban areas. The focus given to communication in local tongue broadly suggests the difficulties attached to a newfangled literacy strategy. With a vast arrangement of languages, including regional dialects, how is English ranked in a multi-lingual society? With relation to Pinker's (1994) ideas, is pidgin or creole English more commonly represented as the *lingua franca*? Or is there enough educational structure in place to warrant it as a developing second language? The factors discussed within the literature form the basis of this scoping study into whether or not a phonics programme can assist in the development of English and whether it can fit into the Ghanaian Literacy curriculum?

2.4 Hypothesis

The following hypothesis was considered with relation to other studies of similar nature and academic commendation. It also considers theoretical findings and contemporary arguments that feature later on in this study (see chapter 2). The hypothesis presented below acknowledges both research questions and was created to work as a conjecture throughout all aspects of the study.

1   There will be a universal agreement around the credibility of a synthetic phonics programme to enhance literacy development within the SCT's constituent area.

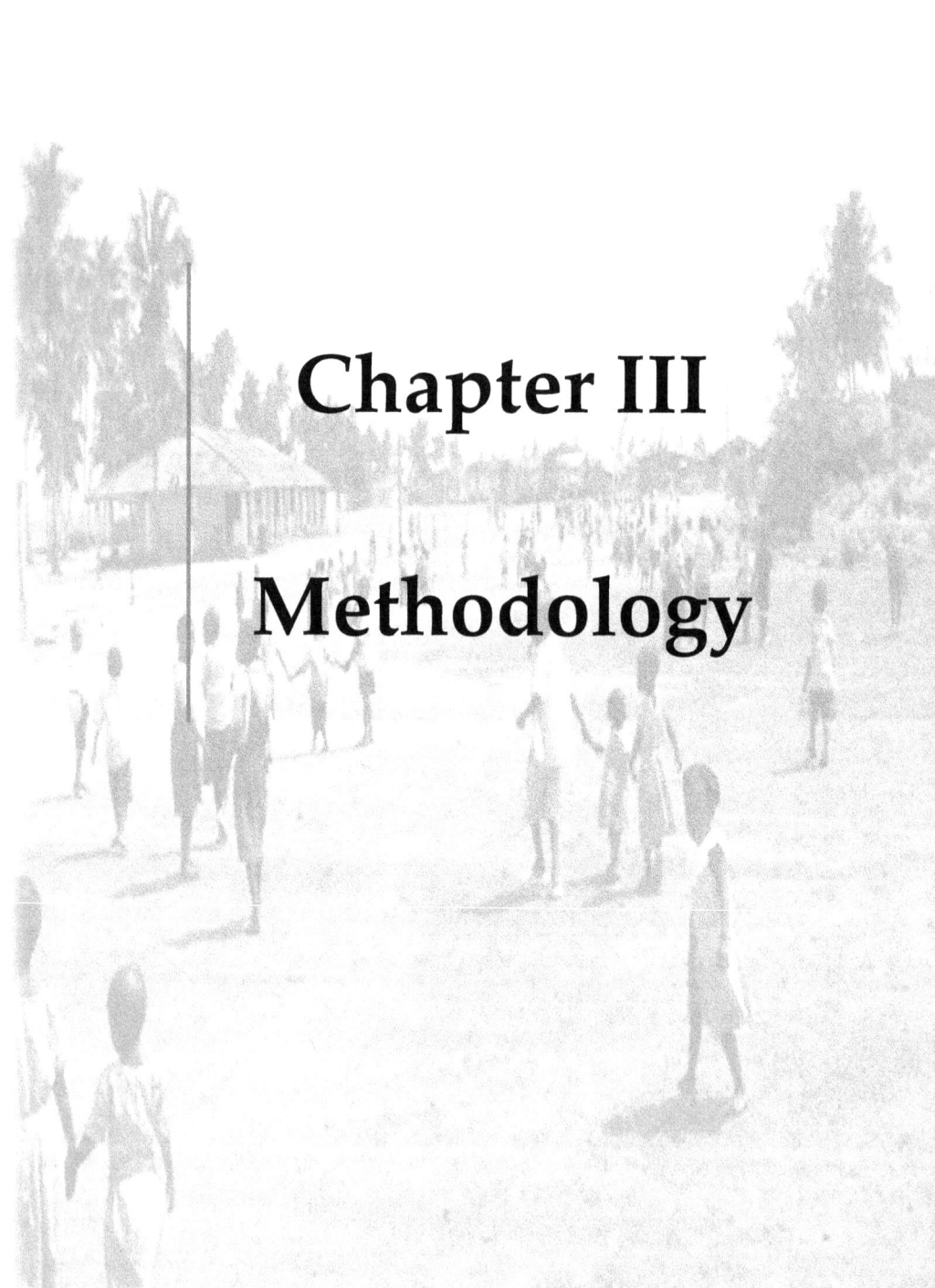

Chapter III

Methodology

Introduction

This chapter outlines the methods used in carrying out the scoping study into perceptions of phonological strategies in rural Ghana's primary schools. More specifically, the chapter will breakdown the preparation of particular methods used and examine why certain choices were made. It should be noted that this study followed an evolutionary scheme which took shape during the collection of data period.

3.1 General Perspectives

As outlined in the proposal, this study involved a single trip to the KEEA district in Ghana. A focus was set to travel to different schools in the area to collect data through the use of a structured questionnaire. However, it was deemed feasible to attract school leaders at the local education authority office to collect the necessary information. Additionally, a semi-structured interview with the education authority, a leading practitioner in one of SCT's partner schools and an early year's teacher was seen as the primary method of data collection.

Context of Study

The context of this study embodies both qualitative and quantitative perspectives to answer the proposed research questions. The following chapters are broken down into qualitative and quantitative sections to enable a detailed analysis to the choices made. For this study, the primary research method was to combine the findings from a semi-structured interview with two professionals working in one of SCT's partner schools and one professional from KEEA's education authority. The ontological scope of this study required a second method to accompany the findings of the primary method. A structured questionnaire provided a practical way of achieving this. The study has acknowledged the merging of both quantitative and qualitative research methods. As a general rule of thumb, this research adopted Morgan's (1997) research design of qualitative primary, quantitative first. The development of this method enabled the researcher to collect qualitative data as a basis for interpreting the quantitative data in the discussion chapter.

3.2 Ethics Considerations

SCT has a long and sustainable partnership with three local schools in the KEEA region, mutual respect from the community and a reciprocal working relationship with the education authority. Hence, a significant amount of care and due diligence was applied to the research phase of this study. With the monolithic emphasis upon traditional values and acculturative norms, the research phase applied cultural intelligence to ensure that all the respondents and community were not perturbed at the gathering of data stage. Given the sensitivity of the collection of research, all participants have remained anonymous in this report and will continue thereafter. Therefore, when reporting the data, names will be exchanged for professional titles. No further publication or re-circulation of this report whether for domestic or international reference will gauge the names of the respondents. Furthermore, the collection of material, handling and transfer of information will not be used to harm the individuals' professional integrity.

With SCT's trust and local connections, it was possible to have full access to all of the schools in the constituent area. Specific measures have been put into place during the pre-research phase of this project. Firstly, SCT sought confirmation of the proposed research; this was discussed on the telephone and through email correspondence with SCT's development director. Secondly, given the nature of the research, all interviewees' and respondents of the questionnaires were told about the actions of the researcher. Thus, all respondents had the choice to participate within this study, a right to withdraw or the right to change ones mind. Each respondent had the opportunity to do this before, during and leading up to the publication of this report.

The research understands the sensitivity around child-led research and the importance of anonymity and child protection. As part of due diligence and school and authority protocol, signing into and out of buildings were recorded when collecting information. This was setup by the request of the head teacher and leading figures within the local education authority in KEEA.

3.3 Qualitative Method

KEEA Education Authority Demographics

Geographically located in the small town of Elmina, the KEEA education authority comprises of twelve administration offices, with four rooms dedicated to specialised year groups and subject areas. In its broadest terms, the KEEA education authority represents 48 schools in the catchment area (Komenda/Edina/Eguafo/Abirem-ghanadistricts.gov.org). The authority classifies itself as one of 39 districts that is categorised as being deprived (*ibid*). The authority acknowledges that there has been a huge enrolment into schools since the abolition of school levies (*ibid*). For the purpose of extended study, the office is open Monday to Friday, between 7am to 4pm. This doesn't include holiday periods and is subject to change.

Primary School Demographics

The primary school is located in the village of Brenu Akyinium, which is located approximately 120 miles west of Accra. For the purpose outlined in the ethical considerations the school and the teachers remain anonymous and will be referred to by their professional titles. The demographics of the school include the following:

- Enrolment exceeds 150 students.

- KG, JHS year groups.

- One qualified teacher and 8 non qualified teachers, or in training.

- The community and school socio-economical status is classified as an area of deprivation as recognised by the GES.

Participation

Prior to departure it was originally planned to involve SCT's development director to assist with the interview process. Due to time constraints with other programmes the participation of SCT's development director was restricted to phone conversations about possible questions and suggestions to ascertain the required information.

The interviews were set up through SCT's partnership with the KEEA education authority and the primary schools it serves. This has been maintained since 2004 from the reciprocal working ethos that SCT has built with the authority and their partner schools.

In consideration of possible interviewee targets, the following descriptions were considered to narrow possible candidates to participate in the interviews:

- An Interest in linguistic design, particularly the teaching aspects associated with phonology.

- A leader from an educational environment where practice can be managed and possibly implemented.

- Senior leadership role (government or regional figure) to generate local or national perspectives.

- A leading practitioner to assist at programme level to advance pedagogy.

In accordance with the above description, the following candidates were chosen to participate in the interview process:

- Head teacher of a primary school from the village of Brenu Akyinim

- A KG teacher from the same primary school in Brenu Akyinim

- A literacy Co-ordinator from the KEEA education authority.

The literacy co-ordinator is a qualified primary teacher who has worked for over 15 years in the KEEA district. The literacy co-ordinating job was initially created to help local businesses communicate with businesses from Accra. The role, since the educational reforms, is now applied to educational agendas that cover the new early year's curriculum.

The head teacher is a relatively new to the field of leadership and is also a qualified teacher. The head teacher works closely with the KEEA education authority and SCT to develop educational initiatives and implement up-to-date programmes. The school benefits from ethical volunteers from a variety of international countries, under the supervision of SCT.

The KG teacher is currently the only fully qualified teacher in the school (apart from the head). The KG teacher has two years of experience in the teaching profession and has studied phonics as part of an initial teacher training programme.

With the acceptance of the literacy coordinator from KEEA, the head teacher and KG teacher participate in the interview, and the planning stage of constructing relevant questions began. Whilst in the country, SCT's country manager helped to recognise recent local developments and up-to-date literature that supported the planning of the interview process.

Instruments Used to Collect Data

A number of instruments were used before and during the recording process of the interview. Firstly, a predetermined list of questions was set out on a piece of A4 paper to assist and guide the interviews. It should be noted that during the interview, impulse questions were asked to help develop an answer. The use of a dictaphone was used to record the conversation and to support the writing process. This technique has been particularly reliable for editing the prolix responses. The limitations of the dictaphone included being unable to record non-verbal empathetic responses. The written process, using a predetermined code of practice was able to record these actions and is discussed later in the analysis of data section. All the recorded information on the dictaphone was then transcribed using MS Word's built in transcriber. This was then edited with predetermined codes to produce the final transcript that is included in this study.

Procedural Notifications

Given the nature of this research, an ethics committee sought a proposal before the commencement of the study. Once this was agreed, travel arrangements were made for a visit to the region. It was originally planned to interview the head of English in KEEA to help answer the proposed research questions. However, a request was denied from the office due to regional testing. In contingency, the regional literacy coordinator was targeted as a possible replacement. Communication between the education authority and the country manager established an arrangement of an interview with the literacy coordinator for the area. The arrangement of the interview was only accepted with the condition of the articles that can be found overleaf.

i. Anonymity of individual or change of name.

ii. No photographs or video of the individual or building (this included all offices and buildings listed as property of the Ghanaian Government).

iii. Printed copies of documents shall not be published without consent.

iv. No unauthorised copy of government documents (includes local and national statistics).

v. All carried items shall receive a thorough examination before and after entry to the building.

Communication between the country manager and the authority further allowed the acceptance of a dicataphone on the premises, with the recommendation detailed below:

i. Any recording device (including a Dictaphone) will be only accepted via the clearance of article (V).

Data Analysis

The qualitative raw data gathered from all the interviews were transcribed using a MS Word's built in transcribers interface. The series of questions were broken down into three clusters. Table 1.1 details the clusters and produces the descriptions of how each of the interviews developed.

Table 1.1 Categories of Questions

Cluster Name	Description
General	To settle the interviewee. Warm up questions.
Educational Provision	To understand the factors that might affect the research questions.
Phonological	To answer both the research questions

Table 1.1 presents the cluster of questions as a simple way to trace the meanings behind the categories. The grouping of questions enabled the first stage of reducing the raw data in preparation of a cross analysis study of all the interview transcripts.

The transcribing of data used a set way to encompass the utterances and track the non-verbal communication used by the respondents. The method is adapted from Gywn's (2002) transcription symbols. Table 1.2 produces the symbols that were included in the production of the transcripts.

Table 1.2 Transcription Symbols

SYMBOL	DESCRIPTION
(.)	Less than 1 second
_ _ _ / _ _ _ _ _ _	Name of a place or person that requires protecting
!!!!	Animated utterance
?	Question
(3.0)	Length of longer pauses
("unintelligent")	If no words can be discerned
(laughing)	Non-verbal sound

Once all interviews were transcribed, each interview was read on numerous occasions to scout for patterns and similarities in the responses. This produced the core of a cross analysis of all three interviews. With the dissected information broken into three sections, a number of themes emerged that reoccurred frequently in the transcripts. Diagram 1.3 presents the acquisition of narrative method, which was used to extract the themes. The discovery of the themes re-engaged the exploration into the narrative. Indeed, this was not the primary method of extracting the data. However, this choice was made at the comparative stage, to present the data in a logical thematic scheme. This can be viewed and is further discussed in the next chapter.

Diagram 1.3 Acquisition of Themes

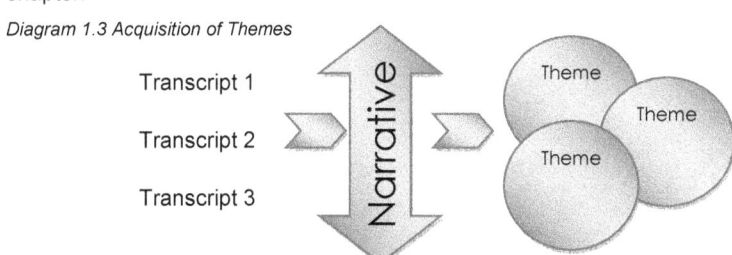

All the themes related back to its derived category (as seen in table 1.1). This enabled the coded responses to be tracked and cross referenced against the opposing data from the other transcripts. Therefore, when the same questions were asked to all the participants, each answer was analysed and compared with the resulting summary at the end.

3.4 Quantitative Method

Context

The second phase of the study focused on collecting questionnaires from school leaders who were situated at the local education office during the initial research trip. The aim of the questionnaire was to support the qualitative data that was collected from the interviews. It represented a feasible way of collecting secondary evidence in conjunction with the primary method.

Participants and Distribution

To give the study scope, 15 schools were initially targeted within a 20 mile radius of the KEEA education headquarters. Due to time constraints, the study selected 8 out of the 15 chosen schools. No schools were chosen because of educational performance. Table 1.1 identifies the selection process through educational similarity. Therefore, the following 8 schools were picked because of the early year's provision that was in place. This selection process of the schools was vital to extract the necessary information. If the study was repeated it could be argued, to give a true picture of the holistic view of the district, all schools would need to participate.

Table 1.4 Educational Provision Similarities

School 1	School 2	School 3	School 4	School 5	School 6	School 7	School 8
Primary only	KG, Primary	Primary only	Primary, JHS, SSS	KG only	KG, Primary	KG, Primary, JHS	KG, Primary

The preliminary study helped to identify and address any ambiguous questions and uncertainty. By formatting the questionnaire into sections, the findings will be that similar to the pre-coded responses technique that was used in the interview.

Design

The questionnaire was written with regard to five themes that related to the educational provision of the schools. The study had no professional attachment, no statistical material and no other preliminary data about the schools before the questionnaire was dispatched. The need to understand the culture of the school benefited the research and facilitated the thematic layout of the questionnaire. Table 1.1 illustrates the 5 themes that formed the focus of answering the research questions.

Table 1.5 Thematic Divisions

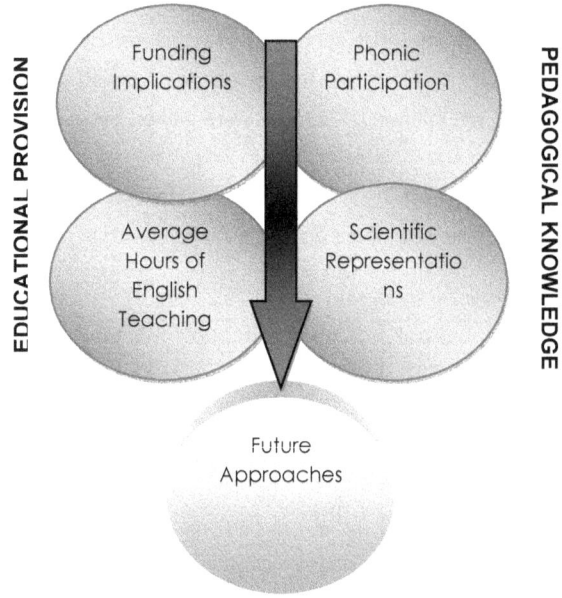

Each theme is layered to best answer the research questions. In general terms the questionnaire was split into two categories. Firstly, it wanted to understand if there were any provisional constraints to the development of educational strategies.

Secondly, the questionnaire gauged the thoughts of the professional's knowledge of phonology, with links to the scientific techniques in its delivery. With direct association to the questionnaire format, questions 1-6 place an emphasis upon understanding the educational demographics of the schools. Questions 7- 11 concentrated on the scientific knowledge of the schools, and their views around phonologic pedagogy. Finally, questions 12 and 13 were written to understand more about the decisions that will be considered for future practice. The format of the questionnaire can be viewed at the back of this report.

The division of such themes enabled a better coding response and a comparable analysis in each category. The findings are illustrated in the presentation of data chapter.

Summary

The information in this chapter has provided the methods used in this qualitative primary, quantitative first study. It tracked the research stages that developed before the data collection period. The next chapter presents the results that were obtained using both methods.

Chapter IV

Presentation of Results

4.1 Qualitative Collections

The following information was collected from interviews that were conducted with three educational professionals from the KEEA district. The presentation of data follows a cross-analysis of particular re-occurring themes taken from the transcripts.

Many themes emerged from the interviews that explored different areas of Ghanaian culture and its link to educational values. Out of the seven possible themes that emerged, four themes appeared to be in common across all of the interviewees' responses. Table 1.6 displays all the themes that came from the interview transcripts with the re-occurring points that are underlined below.

Table 1.6 Major and Re-occurring Themes

THEMES
Fante as the social and educational language of the early years
Family focus on work rather than education
Children staying in school
Unstructured lessons
Financial restrictions on schools
The science of phonics as a development tool for practice
Too many children, not enough schools

Each theme in table 1.6 should not be viewed as a hierarchy of severity. Indeed, there is a similarity of each theme that is associated to the answers given from each respondent. Further analysis of each theme is worthy of new study that surrounds each phenomenon, but goes beyond the planned research searchlight, paying particular regard to the proposed research questions.

Interview Analysis

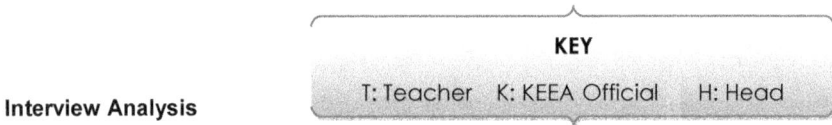

KEY

T: Teacher   K: KEEA Official   H: Head

Throughout the process of searching through the thematic division (as seen in table 1.5 and produced in table 1.6), the idea of content-analyses, which is often used to quantify findings in psychoanalytical research, was partly used due to the similar responses in the interviews. This study uses the responses in a qualitative arrangement when producing the findings. The choice to produce the findings using this technique engages the reader with the responses. It may or may not have empathetic links, but the realism of the content will shape thinking about each theme. It should be noted that it was virtually impossible to include the detailed transcripts in this publication given the mass of data collected. Instead, using the searchlight method and guided by the cross-core analysis, similar outputs were recognised and are detailed below.

From the interviews, the continual reference to Fante as the social and instructional language featured throughout as a focal point of reference in all the transcripts. It represented the habitual delivery of communication within the KEEA district. T: cites it as *"the language of meaning"*. K: identified the developmental link as *"Fante is the language of early childhood"*. H: supplemented the findings by stating *"Without Fante there would be Twi, Ewe or some other language ahead of English"*. In summary, the order of primary and secondary language is addressed as Fante first, English second. From this, the findings project the unpopularity and idle usage of the language in the early years as heavily underused and redundant. The educational link with such claims is described by K: as *"Children learn in Fante with their friends and teacher singing, jumping and playing in the sand"*. T: echoed similar claims by suggesting, *"English is impossible to learn before Fante, for small children"*. Both comments suggest children's linguistic development is heavily dependant upon

Fante. For these reasons it can be concluded that an English programme in the early years could distract learning and cause confusion. The scientific evidence to such claims is discussed with relation to the empiric findings in the next chapter. All of the respondents agreed that the provision of early years was influenced by the decisions taken by the head teacher. The head teacher acknowledged this by confirming these points in the job specification question. Two points arose from the transcripts that developed the knowledge of why there was no structured English teaching in the KG years. Firstly, H: stated that *"Teachers needed in primary year groups, more studies and development"*. A similar response was echoed by T: *"Too many children in KG years to teach English"*. Both responses indicate a resource problem in the early years. With financial restrictions and lack of government funding to recruit teachers for a particular programme is problematic for the school in question.

The third theme that emerged was the similar phonologic links Fante has with English. All respondents agreed there were similarities in the methodological strategies imposed upon the teaching of Fante. However, this wasn't developed further with regard to a potential programme for English. The transcripts detail varying responses concerning this issue. The practice of phonology as a linguistic approach to developing language was initially not understood. This was particularly reported between the scientific classification of analytic and synthetic approaches. However, with further inquiry, a parallel link between phonological strategies and the development of practice was recognised from the transcript. T: explained, *"Children from KG sound letters and write them onto board"*. H: gave a detailed answer by explaining the process *"KG is for children to see letter for first time; children will sort the letter by making different sounds. Children will make word from all sound and learn new word each time"*. This was mirrored by K: *"Sound each letter to help understand the letter before word, children see letter before word, word come later after all word can be used"*. All descriptions are detailed enough to support a claim of a synthetic phonics programme in operation. The findings also suggest that there are certain similarities between English and Fante.

4.2 Quantitative Collections

The following information was collected from questionnaires that were conducted from eight schools in the KEEA district (see appendices for questionnaire). The following presentation of data produces a comparison of results found in this study.

The first section of the questionnaire was written to understand more about the school's demographic situation. Seven out of the eight schools reported to have a full time head teacher, one school reported only having a deputy head.

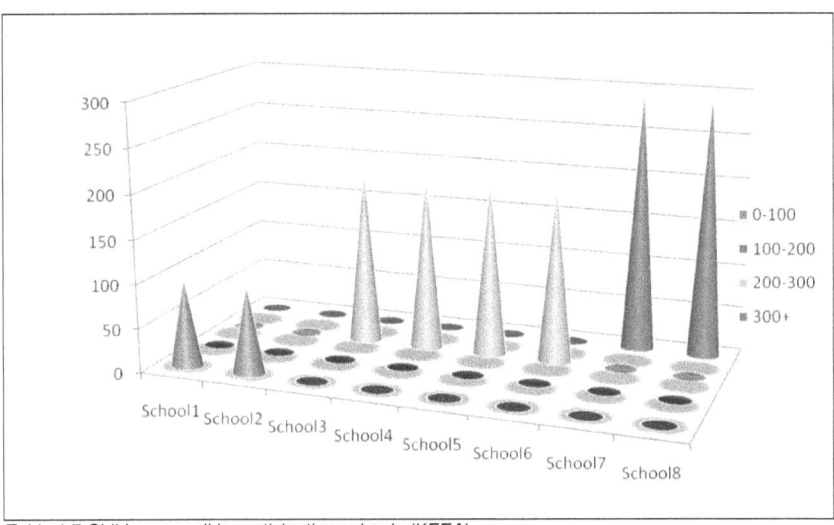

Table 1.7 Children on roll in participating schools (KEEA).

The findings from question two suggest that out of the eight schools that participated in the questionnaire, four out of eight of them showed to have between 200 and 300 pupils attending school. Only two schools in the area have over 300 plus pupils, similarly only two out of eight have less than 100.

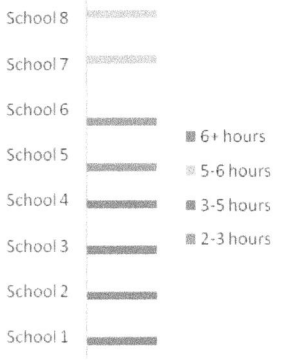

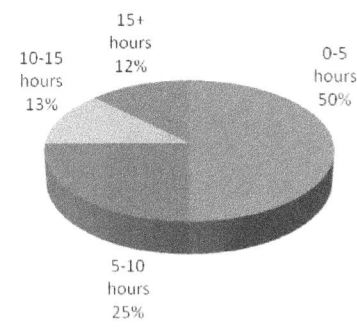

Table 1.8 Hours in school day   Table 1.9 Hours of English teaching (week)

Table 1.8 provides the number of hours in a school day. The findings from the table suggest that four out of eight schools operate between 3-5 hours. This is supplemented by two schools that operate between 5-6 hours and two other schools operating between 2-3 hours.

The results from Table 1.9 indicate that 50% of schools allocate between 0-5 hours of English teaching a week. In addition, it also finds that 25% teach up to 5-10 hours a week. By amalgamating the tables, deeper analysis of the results can be produced. If the findings were considered with their highest value (i.e., 5 out of 0-5, or 6 out of 5-6) the majority of the findings would suggest that for a school that runs for 3-5 hours a day, will only dedicate one hour of English teaching per day. This equates to five hours a week teaching time in a 25 hour school week.

From the findings in Table 2.1, there were 63% of schools disclosing that there were still payments outstanding from National Funding. In contrast only 12% of schools acknowledged full payment. Table 2.2 highlights that 50% of schools begin teaching English from the beginning of the first year of the Primary phase. With 37% beginning in the KG phase. More alarmingly is the 13% of schools that don't teach the language. A brief summary from both charts points to the lack of funding to start English in the early years. This is explored further in the next chapter.

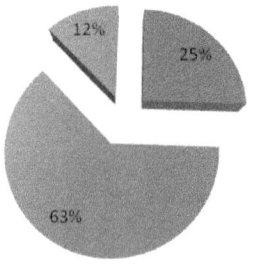

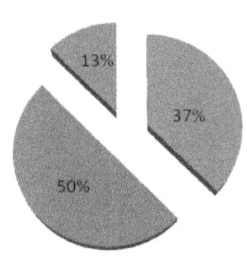

Table 2.1 National Funding   *Table 2.2 English first taught (in year groups)*

Questions seven and eight wanted to determine whether a phonics programme was running in the schools and whether it was part of a syllabus. Table 2.3 acknowledges that 63% of schools do run a phonics programme. However, from Table 2.4 the findings suggest that there is no structure to the programme. The results also show a pattern. Whilst there is a programme in place in the majority of schools, the evidence suggests that this may indeed be a self-tailored programme.

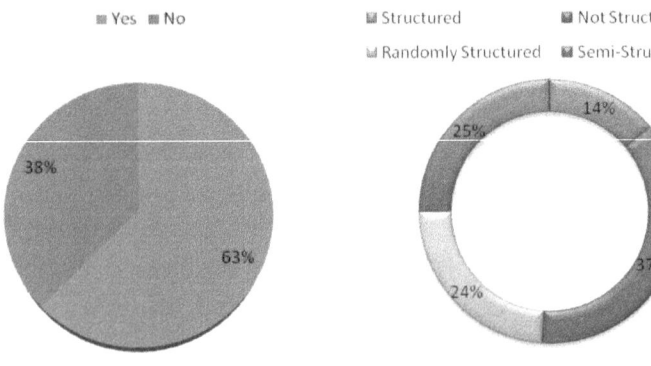

Table 2.3 Runs a phonic programme   *Table 2.4 Type of phonic programme*

Questions nine to eleven aimed to understand more about the practice that operates in the schools. Table 2.5 represents the findings from question nine that found 38% of schools were not sure what type of phonics programme they were running with. The findings confirm what was found in table 2.4 that the majority of schools had little structure and were not sure about the techniques involved in delivering a structured phonics programme.

Which **best** describes the phonics programme you run in your school?			
Individual letters sounded into words.	Don't run a programme.	Whole words broken up then sounded.	Not sure.
12%	25%	25%	38%

Table 2.5 Best description of the type of phonic programme used in school

Questions ten and eleven built upon the scientific representations of phonology. Both questions were asked to help understand whether schools fully understood the components of what makes a synthetic and analytic phonic programme. Chart 2.6 suggests that 50% of schools thought that this type of programme would be based upon breaking down whole words. This is in fact an incorrect answer, as a synthetic programme is based upon the synthesising of individual phonemes to produce CVC and CVCC words. From the results, only 12% of schools made a correct link to the right answer. Question eleven followed a similar format, it asked about the analytic components of a programme. It was found that 38% of schools thought the answer to be linked to the blending of phonemes. Interestingly, 25% matched the correct answer by stating that analytic phonic components were represented by the breakdown of words. Therefore, 75% of schools were not able to answer this correctly which mirrored the findings from question ten. From both findings there is evidence to support a better need to understand the scientific purposes of both disciplines.

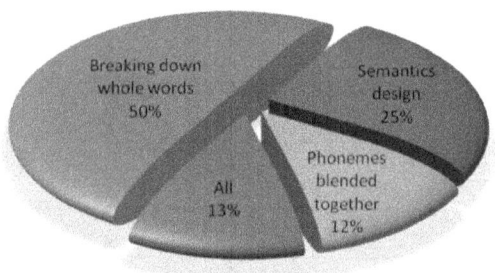

The final two questions provided an insight into the future of phonological strategies into the schools that participated in the study. Chart 2.7 merges the findings from questions twelve and thirteen from the questionnaire. It illustrates that 50% of schools would prefer a synthetic approach to the teaching of phonics.

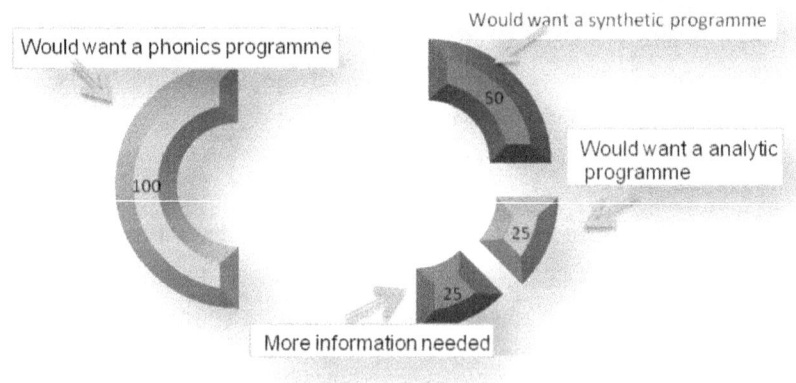

Chart 2.7 Analysis of Programme Type

By comparison, the results from chart 2.6 suggest that only 12% of schools understand the true meaning of this method. Further analysis shows that chart 2.7 justifies the need to understand more about each programme, this was acknowledged by 25% of the respondents.

Chapter V

Discussion

5.1 Discussion of Quantitative and Qualitative Data

From the beginning, the study was driven by two research questions that assayed the perceptions of a potential phonics programme to run in a rural village in Ghana. It also wanted to gauge professional opinion to which programme would be seen as the primary pedagogy. This section will discuss the findings according to each of the research questions. It will analyse in detail with direct reference to the theoretical evidence stated previously in the literature.

Research Question 1

From the gathered data, there is overwhelming evidence to support a claim that an English phonics programme is a favoured pedagogy amongst the professionals featured in this study. The findings from both the quantitative and qualitative data produce a claim that through a structured programme, children will naturally benefit linguistically throughout their educational lives. From the points discussed in this study and with regard to the empirical and theoretical studies found in the literature; there is an unequivocal notion that if children are exposed to English (if this is not the instructional language) in the KG years, then it is far more likely they will develop the core linguistic skills needed to succeed in the higher years.

The qualitative and quantitative evidence draw similar conclusions to the first research question posed. Both the interviews and questionnaires repeatedly found problems of why learning English in the early years has not yet been mandatory. The common theme across the findings pointed to the potential of learning both languages at the same time can be harmful for children's development. From the literature, there is evidence from Chomsky and Halle's (1968) findings to suggest given the universality of generative grammar, children who become exposed early to a second language will have a deeper and better understanding of it. However, this alone isn't the primary reason, with cognition and social constructivists playing an equally important role. Piaget's belief of a language being learned through environmental factors is cited as the main example of this movement. As mentioned earlier, the difference between urban and rural educational institutions places the environment as a key factor when considering linguistic attainment (see Huber,

1999, Salm & Falola, 2002). Conclusively, both scientific approaches, although opposing the centrality of the language acquisition argument, support a claim that children's language development is dependant on the enrichment of early experiences. Therefore, an accompanied English programme will help to improve children's language development. If children are not structurally exposed to Fante and English in the early years, the generative lexicon may indeed be more complexly formed. Pinker's (1994) ideas also raised questions in connection with this study as to providing a realistic answer to why children struggle with English in the later years of education. With the developing years vital to children's pre-linguistic to natural linguistic development, Pinker's (1994) ideas of pidgin to creole English is recognised as a potential barrier to achievement. As highlighted previously in the literature, the construction of this theory relates to the way children will merge native languages with second languages. The implications of educational development rests upon the generative terms already pre-absorbed from earlier teachings.

Research Question 2

The findings from this study recognised the national view of limited access to learn English in the early years, as originally reported by Annan (2004). Two main themes emerged as probable causation of why this is the trend. Firstly, the schools sampled in the questionnaire indicated a problem with fiscal arrangements to fund teaching places and educational programmes. The literature cites the FCUBE programme to be the driver of educational initiatives and holistic provision in Ghana (Commission, 2007). Without systematic payments to support such schemes, schools and districts will not be able to maintain educational structure.

From this study, it was found that most professionals sampled from the interviews and questionnaires did not understand the scientific development of language. This is identified with the scientific classification of the two pedagogical types of phonology. Analytic and synthetic approaches were misunderstood and underdeveloped with reference to practice. However, the main finding from this study broadly suggests that a synthetic programme would be more useful because of the way children learn individual letters from their instructional language. Similar findings were found in the Clackmannanshire study in Scotland that advocated synthetic phonics as the main approach of delivery (see SOEID, 1998). However, phonological didactics is not recognised in Ghana as a method of improving literacy. With relation to the literature, it is acknowledged from the Rose Review that children, by the age of five should be receiving at least 20 minutes a day of phonics (see DfES,2006, Ward, 2009). The Rose Review also mentioned initial teacher training as a method to raise awareness of such approaches (ibid). Whilst the topic of teacher training didn't emerge in this study, it offers a point of discussion that signifies the importance of advancing the knowledge of scientific linguistic pedagogy.

.

Chapter VI

Conclusion

6.1Summary of Findings

This scoping study into the perceptions of phonology from professionals working in educational settings has found a potential barrier to learning English in the early years. It has been discovered through this study that professionals would welcome a structured synthetic phonics programme to support the development of English in the early years. However, the study acknowledges the regional and national factors that may hinder the future of such a programme. With consideration to the hypothesis, the instauration of a synthetic phonics programme was correctly predicted as a method to improve children's linguistic development.

Recommendations

The following is a set of recommendations that manifested from the data collected in this study. All the recommendations pertain to this study with acknowledgement of the theoretical and empirical findings. The points below depict the basic requirements that underpin the success of language acquisition and linguistic development from the research that was found in this study. For children to develop linguistically in the early years of education, it is recommended that:

- A structured synthetic phonics programme that gives every child the chance to develop a basic foundation of English that can be maintained and further developed.

- A structured synthetic phonics programme that can be sustained and complement the curriculum timetable.

- A structured synthetic phonics programme that is heavily involved with children's social, emotional and creative environments.

- A structured synthetic phonics programme that shares the value of Ghanaian culture.

Limitations and Scope for Repeat Study

The present study was conducted through gauging the professional opinions of practitioners who work in early year's education in rural Ghana. Due to time constraints, it was unconceivable to travel to every school in the KEEA district. Whilst the study finds a common denominator in favour of a synthetic phonics programme from the participative schools, the study would have greatly benefited from an overall perspective from every school in KEEA.

The interview process could have been improved if there had been more time to develop all the answers to the questions. While the process ran smoothly for all three interviews, being able to exchange confidently in English seemed to put pressure on the respondents. Also, the process would have benefited from shorter questions, especially when dealing with answers that need theoretical or scientific input. The interviews failed to ask about individual school or regional educational performance. At the time, the decision not to ask for statistical information was down to the fact that the figures were potentially unreliable.

The questionnaire in this study asked different questions to the questions asked in the interviews. For the benefit of decoding the data, having the same questions as the interview, with the idea of a semi-structured questionnaire, will largely produce a qualitative study. The advantages of this method will bring together a deeper cross analysis of opinions, rather than predetermined answers that feature in this study.

Listed below are three general points that could recognisably impact the findings:

- A preference to communicate in mother tongue.
- Schools with financial problems may accept an external programme as a way to save money on teaching costs.
- Educational bias of particular programmes.

Suggestions for Further Research

Other issues that arose throughout the course of study that may follow a research thread included:

In terms of local and national movements:

- A review of English development in the early years.
- Early year's teacher training.
- The phonetic instruction of Fante.

Other provision that sits on the boundaries of national and local provision:

- Emotional and social development factors in the shaping of curricula activities.
- Special educational needs requirements and inclusive measures for accessibility to English and other curricula activities.
- Understanding the role of senior leadership in educational settings.

REFERENCES

Agawu. V.K. (2003). *Representing African Music.* London. Routledge.

Ammon. U. Dittmar N. Mattheier. K.J. Trudgill. P (2006). *Sociolinguistics: an international handbook of the science of language and society.* New York. Walter de Gruyter.

Anderson, J. M., & Ewen C. J. (1987). *Principles of dependency phonology.* U.K.. Cambridge University Press.

Arnett. J.J. (2007). *International Encyclopedia of Adolescence: A Historical and Cultural Survey of Young People Around the World.* USA. CRC Press.

Ayshe T. O. Ap E. (2005). *Child Development and Teaching Young Children.* London. Thomson Learning Nelson.

Bissex. G. (1980). *GNYS AT WRK: A Child Learns to Write and Read.* Cambridge. MA: Harvard University Press.

Bohannon, J.N. (1993). *Theoretical approaches to language acquisition.* New York. Macmillan.

Brooks, G. (2002) "Phonemic awareness is a key factor in learning to be literate: how best should it be taught?" In, Cook, M. *Perspectives on the Teaching and Learning of Phonics.* Royston. Herts. UK Reading Association. pp. 61-83.

Cattell. R. (2004). *Children's Language.* New York. Continuum International Publishing Group

Carroll. E. S. (2001). *Input and Evidence: The Raw Material of Second Language Acquisition.* Netherlands. John Benjamins Publishing Company.

Canagarajah, S. & Coulombe, H. (1997) *Child Labor and Schooling in Ghana.* African Region. World Bank,Human Development Technical Family.

Chew. J. (1997). *"Traditional phonics: What it is and what it is not"* Journal of Research in Reading, 20 (3): pp171-83.

Chomsky, N. (1972). *Language and mind.* New York: Praeger.

Chomsky, N., Halle, M. (1968). *The Sound Pattern of English.* New York. Harper & Row.

Chomsky. N. Otero. C.P. (2004). *Language and Politics.* Second Edition. New York. AK Press

Cook. M. (2002). Perspectives *on the Teaching and Learning of Phonics. Royston.* Herts.UK Reading Association.

Cove. M. (2006). "Sounds Familiar: The History of Phonics Teaching", in Lewis. M. Ellis. S. *Phonics Practice, Research and Policy.* London. Sage. pp. 105-114.

CRIQPEG. (1995) *Phase 2 Report,* Ghana, UCC/ILP.

Dakabu. M. (1988). *The Languages of Ghana.* USA. Taylor and Francis.

Dei. G. (2004). *Schooling and Education in Africa: The Case of Ghana.* New Jersey. USA. Africa World Press.

DES. (1975). *A Language for Life.* London. HMSO.

De Villiers J.D. & De Villiers P.A. (1978) *Early Language.* London. Fontana.

DfEE. (1998). *National Literacy Strategy Framework forTeaching.* Stationery Office. HMSO.

DfEE. (1998b). *Literacy Training Pack.* London. HMSO.

DfEE. (1999a). *Progression in Phonics.* London. HMSO

DfES (1998). *The National Literacy Strategy.* Stationery Office. HMSO.

DfES. (2003a). *Playing With Sounds. A Supplement to Progression in Phonics.* London. DfES.

DfES. (2005a). *Independent Review of The Teaching of Early Reading: Interim Report to DfES.* London. DfES.

DfES. (2006). *Independent Review of the Teaching of Early Reading.* (The Rose Review). London. DfES.

Diack. H. (1965). *In Spite of The Alphabet: A Study of the Teaching of Reading.* London. Chatto & Watson.

Dreze, J. & Kingdon, G. G. (2001) School Participation in Rural India. *Review of Development Economics*, 5 (1), 1-24.

Fennell. S. Arnot. M. (2007). *Gender Educational and Equality in a Global Context.* London. Routledge.

Field. J. (2003). *Psycholinguistics.* London. Routledge.

Filmer, D. & Pritchett, L. (1999) The Effect of Household Wealth on Educational Attainment: Evidence from 35 Countries. *Population and Development Review*, 25 (1), 85-120.

Gentry. R. (1982). "An Analysis in Developmental Spelling in GNYS AT WRK", *The Reading Teacher.* 36: pp192-200.

Government of Ghana (GOG), (2004) *White Paper on the Report of the Education Reform Review Committee.* Accra. Ministry of Education Youth and Sports.

Goodman. S. Lillis. T. Maybin. J. Mercer. J. (2003). *Language, Literacy and Education: A Reader.* London. Trentham Books.

Goldsmith. J.A. (1999). *Phonological Theory: The Essential Readings.* London. Blackwell Publishing.

Graham. C.K. (1971). *The History of Education in Ghana: From the Earliest Times to the Declaration of Independence.* London. Frank Cass.

Gross, R. (1999) *Psychology: The Science of Mind and Behaviour.* (3rd Edition). London. Hodder and Stoughton

Gwyn. J. (2002). *Communicating Health and Illness.* London. Sage.

Hall. K. (2006). "How Children Learn to Read and How Phonics Helps", in Lewis. M. Ellis. S. *Phonics Practice, Research and Policy*. London. Sage. pp10.

Hall, N, Marsh, J (2003) *Handbook of Early Literacy*, London, SAGE.

Hanna. R. (2006). *Rationality and Logic*. USA. MIT Press.

House of Commons Education and Skills Committee. (2005). *Teaching Children to Read*. 8TH Report of the Session, 2004-05. London. The Stationery Office.

Huber. M. (1999). *Ghanaian Pidgin English in it's West African Context*. USA. John Benjamin Publishing.

Huxford. L. (2006). "Phonics in Context: Spelling Links", in, Lewis. M. Ellis. S. *Phonics Practice, Research and Policy*. London. Sage. pp85.

Hymes, D (1972) "On Communicative Competence", in, Pride. J.B. Holmes. J. *Sociolinguistics*. Harmondsworth. Penguin.

Johnston. R.S. Watson. J.E. (2004). Accelerating the development of reading, spelling and phonemic awareness skills in initial readers, Reading and Writing: *An Interdisciplinary Journal*, 17(4): pp327-57.

Komenda/Edina/Eguafo/Abirem (2006).*About Komenda/ Edina/ Eguafo/ Abirem.* [Internet]. Available at: http://keea.ghanadistricts.gov.gh/. (Accessed 10th November 2008).

Labov. W. (1972). *The Transformation of Experience in Narrative Syntax. Language in the inner cities*. Philadelphia. Universtiy of Pennsylvania Press.

Little. A. (2007). *Education for All Multigrade Teaching*. USA. Springer.

Macmillian. B. (2002). "Rhyme and Reading: A critical review of the research methodology", in, *Journal of Research in Reading*. 25 (1): pp4-42.

Maitland. L.L. Hannah. P. (2007). *5 Steps to a 5 AP Psychology: 2008-2009 Edition.* (2nd Edition). London. McGraw-Hill Professional.

Mallet. M. (2008). The *Primary English Encyclopedia: The Heart of the Curriculum*. London. Routledge.

Mansour. G. (1993). *Multilingualism and Nation Building*. UK. Multilingual Matters and Channel View Publishing.

Ministry of Education, Science and Sports (1996). *Towards Learning for All: Basic Education in Ghana to the year 2000*. Accra. Ministry of Education.

Ministry of Education (1999*): A Background Paper prepared for the Ministry of Education: National Education Forum*. Accra: Ministry of Education

Ministry of Education, Science and Sports (2000). *Policies and Strategic Plan 2001-2003 for the Education Sector Pre-Tertiary*. Accra. Ministry of Education.

Ministry of Education, Science and Sports. (2006). *Preliminary Education Sector Performance Report*. Accra: Ministry of Education

Naylor. G. (2000). *Ghana*. London. Oxfam Publishing.

Nesin. J. Omatseye. B. (2008). *Going to School in Sub-Saharan Africa*. USA. Greenwood. Press.

Newell. S. (2002). *Literary Culture in Colonial Ghana*. Manchester. Manchester University Press.

Oates. J. Grayson. A. (2004). *Cognitive and Language Development in Children*. UK. Blackwell Publishing.

Obeng. S. Hartford. B. (2002). *Political independence with linguistic servitude*. Indianna. Nova Publishers.

Ofsted. (2001). *Teaching of Phonics:* London. HMSO

Ofsted (2002) The *National Literacy Strategy: the first four years 1998-2002*. London: Office for Standards in Education.

Owen, R.E. (1988). *Language development: An introduction* (2nd ed.), Ohio. Merrill Publishing.

Piatelli-Palmarini, M. (1980). *Language and Learning. The Debate Between Jean Piaget and Noam Chomsky.* London: Routledge & Kegan Paul

Pinker. S. (1994). *The Language Instinct.* University Of California. Morrow & Company Publishers.

Read. C. (1986). *Children's Creative Spelling.* London. Routledge.

Rogoff. B. (2003). *The cultural Nature of Human Development.* New York. Oxford University Press.

Rolleston. C. (2009). *Educational Access and Exclusion: The Case of Ghana 1991-2006.* Brighton. University of Sussex.

Rosen. M. (2006). "Synthetic Arguments" in, Lewis. M. Ellis. S. *Phonics Practice, Research and Policy.* London. Sage. pp123.

Sabre Charitable Trust (SCT) – Teaching Methodology [Internet]. Available at: http://sabretrust.org/education_teaching.php <Accessed 10th November 2008>

Salm. J. Falola. T. (2002). *Culture and Customs of Ghana.* New York. Greenwood Publishing Group.

SOEID (Scottish Office Education and Industry Department). (1998). *Accelrating Reading Attainment: The Effectiveness of Synthetic Phonics.* Edinburgh: SOEID.

Shaffer, D.R. (1993). *Developmental of Language and Communication Skills: Childhood and Adolescence* (3rd ed).USA. Pacific Grove.

Southgate. V. Roberts. G.R. (1970). *Reading- Which Approach?* London. Unibooks. University of London Press.

Sunal. C. Mutua. K. (2007). *The Enterprise of Education.* USA. Information Age Publishing.

Strauss. S. (2005). *The Linguistics, Neurology, and Politics of Phonics: Silent "E" Speaks Out.* USA. Routledge.

Stuart. M. Materson. J. Dixon. M. Quinlan. P. (1999). "Interacting process in the development of printed word recognition", in, T. Nunes. *Learning to Read: An Integrated View from Research and Practice*. Dordrecht: Kluwer Academic.

Talay-Ongan. A. Ap. E. (2005). *Child Development and Teaching Young Children*. Australia. Thomson Learning Nelson.

Torgesen. C. Brooks. G. Hall. J. (2006) *"A Systematic Review of the Research Literature on the Use of Phonics in the Teaching of Reading and Spelling"*. Research Report 711. London. DfES. pp47-50.

Wan. G. (2008). *The Education of Diverse Student Populations: A Global Perspective*. USA. Springer.

Ward. H. (2009). *Synthetic phonics are bringing real rewards*. [Internet]. Available at: http://www.tes.co.uk/article.aspx?storycode=6007895 <Accessed 8TH April 2009>

Wyse. D. (2006). "Rose-Tinted Spectacles: Synthetic Phonics. Research Evidence and the Teaching of Reading", in, Lewis. M. Ellis. S. *Phonics Practice, Research and Policy*. London. Sage. pp. 125-126.

Wyse. D. Jones. R. Bradford. H. (2006). *Teaching English, Language and Literacy*. London. Routledge.

BIBLIOGRAPHY

Agawu. V.K. (2003). *Representing African Music*. London. Routledge.

Ammon. U. Dittmar N. Mattheier. K.J. Trudgill. P (2006). *Sociolinguistics: an international handbook of the science of language and society*. New York. Walter de Gruyter.

Anderson, J. M., & Ewen C. J. (1987). *Principles of dependency phonology*. U.K.. Cambridge University Press.

Arnett. J.J. (2007). *International Encyclopedia of Adolescence: A Historical and Cultural Survey of Young People Around the World*. USA. CRC Press.

Ayshe T. O. Ap E. (2005). *Child Development and Teaching Young Children*. London. Thomson Learning Nelson.

Bissex. G. (1980). *GNYS AT WRK: A Child Learns to Write and Read*. Cambridge. MA: Harvard University Press.

Bohannon, J.N. (1993). *Theoretical approaches to language acquisition*. New York. Macmillan.

Brooks, G. (2002) "Phonemic awareness is a key factor in learning to be literate: how best should it be taught?", in Cook, M. *Perspectives on the Teaching and Learning of Phonics*. Royston. Herts. UK Reading Association. pp. 61-83.

Cattell. R. (2004). *Children's Language*. New York. Continuum International Publishing Group

Carroll. E. S. (2001). *Input and Evidence: The Raw Material of Second Language Acquisition*. Netherlands. John Benjamins Publishing Company.

Canagarajah, S. & Coulombe, H. (1997) *Child Labor and Schooling in Ghana*. African Region. World Bank,Human Development Technical Family.

Chew. J. (1997). *"Traditional phonics: What it is and what it is not"* Journal of Research in Reading, 20 (3): pp171-83.

Chomsky, N. (1972). *Language and mind*. New York: Praeger.

Chomsky, N., Halle, M. (1968). *The Sound Pattern of English*. New York. Harper & Row.

Chomsky. N. Otero. C.P. (2004). *Language and Politics*. Second Edition. New York. AK Press

Cook. M. (2002). Perspectives *on the Teaching and Learning of Phonics. Royston.* Herts.UK Reading Association.

Cove. M. (2006). "Sounds Familiar: The History of Phonics Teaching", in Lewis. M. Ellis. S. *Phonics Practice, Research and Policy*. London. Sage. pp. 105-114.

CRIQPEG. (1995) *Phase 2 Report*, Ghana, UCC/ILP.

Dakabu. M. (1988). *The Languages of Ghana*. USA. Taylor and Francis.

Dei. G. (2004). *Schooling and Education in Africa: The Case of Ghana*. New Jersey. USA. Africa World Press.

DES. (1975). *A Language for Life*. London. HMSO.

De Villiers J.D. & De Villiers P.A. (1978) *Early Language*. London. Fontana.

DfEE. (1998). *National Literacy Strategy Framework forTeaching*. Stationery Office. HMSO.

DfEE. (1998b). *Literacy Training Pack*. London. HMSO.

DfEE. (1999a). *Progression in Phonics*. London. HMSO

DfES (1998). *The National Literacy Strategy*. Stationery Office. HMSO.

DfES. (2003a). *Playing With Sounds. A Supplement to Progression in Phonics*. London. DfES.

DfES. (2005a). *Independent Review of The Teaching of Early Reading: Interim Report to DfES*. London. DfES.

DfES. (2006). *Independent Review of the Teaching of Early Reading.* (The Rose Review). London. DfES.

Diack. H. (1965). *In Spite of The Alphabet: A Study of the Teaching of Reading.*London. Chatto & Watson.

Dreze, J. & Kingdon, G. G. (2001) School Participation in Rural India. *Review of Development Economics*, 5 (1), 1-24.

Fennell. S. Arnot. M. (2007). *Gender Educational and Equality in a Global Context.* London. Routledge.

Field. J. (2003). *Psycholinguistics.* London. Routledge.

Filmer, D. & Pritchett, L. (1999) The Effect of Household Wealth on Educational Attainment: Evidence from 35 Countries. *Population and Development Review*, 25 (1), 85-120.

Gentry. R. (1982). "An Analysis in Developmental Spelling in GNYS AT WRK", *The Reading Teacher.* 36: pp192-200.

Government of Ghana (GOG), (2004) *White Paper on the Report of the Education Reform Review Committee.* Accra. Ministry of Education Youth and Sports.

Goodman. S. Lillis. T. Maybin. J. Mercer. J. (2003). *Language, Literacy and Education: A Reader.* London. Trentham Books.

Goldsmith. J.A. (1999). *Phonological Theory: The Essential Readings.* London. Blackwell Publishing.

Graham. C.K. (1971). *The History of Education in Ghana: From the Earliest Times to the Declaration of Independence.* London. Frank Cass.

Gross, R. (1999) *Psychology: The Science of Mind and Behaviour.* (3rd Edition). London. Hodder and Stoughton

Gwyn. J. (2002). *Communicating Health and Illness.* London. Sage.

Hall. K. (2006). "How Children Learn to Read and How Phonics Helps", in Lewis. M. Ellis. S. *Phonics Practice, Research and Policy*. London. Sage. pp10.

Hall, N, Marsh, J (2003) *Handbook of Early Literacy*, London, SAGE.

Hanna. R. (2006). *Rationality and Logic*. USA. MIT Press.

Holmes. J. (1972). *Sociolingusitics*. Harmondsworth. Penquin

House of Commons Education and Skills Committee. (2005). *Teaching Children to Read*. 8TH Report of the Session, 2004-05. London. The Stationery Office.

Huber. M. (1999). *Ghanaian Pidgin English in it's West African Context*. USA. John Benjamin Publishing.

Huxford. L. (2006). "Phonics in Context: Spelling Links", in, Lewis. M. Ellis. S. *Phonics Practice, Research and Policy*. London. Sage. pp85.

Hymes, D (1972) "On Communicative Competence", in, Pride. J.B. Holmes. J. *Sociolinguistics*. Harmondsworth. Penguin.

Johnston. R.S. Watson. J.E. (2004). Accelerating the development of reading, spelling and phonemic awareness skills in initial readers, Reading and Writing: *An Interdisciplinary Journal*, 17(4): pp327-57.

Komenda/Edina/Eguafo/Abirem (2006).*About Komenda/ Edina/ Eguafo/ Abirem*. [Internet]. Available at: http://keea.ghanadistricts.gov.gh/. (Accessed 10th November 2008).

Labov. W. (1972). *The Transformation of Experience in Narrative Syntax. Language in the inner cities*. Philadelphia. Universtiy of Pennsylvania Press.

Lewis. M. Ellis. S. (2006). *Phonics Practice, Research and Policy*. London. Sage.

Little. A. (2007). *Education for All Multigrade Teaching*. USA. Springer.

Macmillian. B. (2002). "Rhyme and Reading: A critical review of the research methodology", in, *Journal of Research in Reading*. 25 (1): pp4-42.

Maitland. L.L. Hannah. P. (2007). *5 Steps to a 5 AP Psychology: 2008-2009 Edition.* (2nd Edition). London. McGraw-Hill Professional.

Mallet. M. (2008). The *Primary English Encyclopedia: The Heart of the Curriculum.* London. Routledge.

Mansour. G. (1993). *Multilingualism and Nation Building.* UK. Multilingual Matters and Channel View Publishing.

Ministry of Education, Science and Sports (1996). *Towards Learning for All: Basic Education in Ghana to the year 2000.* Accra. Ministry of Education.

Ministry of Education (1999*): A Background Paper prepared for the Ministry of Education: National Education Forum.* Accra: Ministry of Education

Ministry of Education, Science and Sports (2000). *Policies and Strategic Plan 2001-2003 for the Education Sector Pre-Tertiary.* Accra. Ministry of Education.

Ministry of Education, Science and Sports. (2006). *Preliminary Education Sector Performance Report.* Accra: Ministry of Education

Mutter, V. Hulme, C. Snowling, M (1997). *Phonological Abilities Test (PAT).* London. Harcourt Assessment.

Naylor. G. (2000). *Ghana.* London. Oxfam Publishing.

Nesin. J. Omatseye. B. (2008). *Going to School in Sub-Saharan Africa.* USA. Greenwood. Press.

Newell. S. (2002). *Literary Culture in Colonial Ghana.* Manchester. Manchester University Press.

Nunes. T. (1999). *Learning to Read: An Integrated View from Research and Practice.* Dordrecht. Kluwer Academic.

Oates. J. Grayson. A. (2004). *Cognitive and Language Development in Children.* UK. Blackwell Publishing.

Obeng. S. Hartford. B. (2002). *Political independence with linguistic servitude.* Indianna. Nova Publishers.

Ofsted. (2001). *Teaching of Phonics:* London. HMSO

Ofsted (2002) The *National Literacy Strategy: the first four years 1998-2002.* London: Office for Standards in Education.

Owen, R.E. (1988). *Language development: An introduction* (2nd ed.), Ohio. Merrill Publishing.

Piatelli-Palmarini, M. (1980). *Language and Learning. The Debate Between Jean Piaget and Noam Chomsky.* London: Routledge & Kegan Paul

Pinker. S. (1994). *The Language Instinct.* University Of California. Morrow & Company Publishers.

Read. C. (1986). *Children's Creative Spelling.* London. Routledge.

Rogoff. B. (2003). *The cultural Nature of Human Development.* New York. Oxford University Press.

Rolleston. C. (2009). *Educational Access and Exclusion: The Case of Ghana 1991-2006.* Brighton. University of Sussex.

Rosen. M. (2006). "Synthetic Arguments" in, Lewis. M. Ellis. S. *Phonics Practice, Research and Policy.* London. Sage. pp123.

Sabre Charitable Trust (SCT) – Teaching Methodology [Internet]. Available at: http://sabretrust.org/education_teaching.php <Accessed 10th November 2008>

Salm. J. Falola. T. (2002). *Culture and Customs of Ghana.* New York. Greenwood Publishing Group.

SOEID (Scottish Office Education and Industry Department). (1998). *Accelrating Reading Attainment: The Effectiveness of Synthetic Phonics.* Edinburgh: SOEID.

Shaffer, D.R. (1993). *Developmental of Language and Communication Skills: Childhood and Adolescence* (3rd ed).USA. Pacific Grove.

Southgate. V. Roberts. G.R. (1970). *Reading- Which Approach?* London. Unibooks. University of London Press.

Sunal. C. Mutua. K. (2007). *The Enterprise of Education*. USA. Information Age Publishing.

Strauss. S. (2005). *The Linguistics, Neurology, and Politics of Phonics: Silent "E" Speaks Out*. USA. Routledge.

Stuart. M. Materson. J. Dixon. M. Quinlan. P. (1999). "Interacting process in the development of printed word recognition", in, T. Nunes. *Learning to Read: An Integrated View from Research and Practice*. Dordrecht: Kluwer Academic.

Talay-Ongan. A. Ap. E. (2005). *Child Development and Teaching Young Children*. Australia. Thomson Learning Nelson.

Torgesen. C. Brooks. G. Hall. J. (2006) "*A Systematic Review of the Research Literature on the Use of Phonics in the Teaching of Reading and Spelling*". Research Report 711. London. DfES. pp47-50.

Wan. G. (2008). *The Education of Diverse Student Populations: A Global Perspective*. USA. Springer.

Ward. H. (2009). *Synthetic phonics are bringing real rewards*. [Internet]. Available at: http://www.tes.co.uk/article.aspx?storycode=6007895 <Accessed 8TH April 2009>

Wyse. D. (2006). "Rose-Tinted Spectacles: Synthetic Phonics. Research Evidence and the Teaching of Reading", in, Lewis. M. Ellis. S. *Phonics Practice, Research and Policy*. London. Sage. pp. 125-126.

Wyse. D. Jones. R. Bradford. H. (2006). *Teaching English, Language and Literacy*. London. Routledge.

Appendices

Questionnaire

Please can you answer the following questions as truthfully as possible. The aim of this questionnaire is to understand your views into the themes that are covered below.

Q1.   Which one of the following are you?

Headteacher   Deputy   Lead Teacher   Other (Please Specify)

Q2.   How many children are on roll in your school?

0-100   100-200   200-300   300+

Q3.   How long (in hours) does your school day run for?

2-3   3-5   5-6   6+

Q4.   How many hours a week are dedicated to the teaching of English in your school?

None   5-10   10-15   15+

Q5.   Does your school receive regular Capitation Grant funding as outlined from the FCUBE initiative?

Yes   Funds   Payments   No

                     delayed   outstanding   payments

Q6.   At what grade entry level is English **first** taught in your school?

KG 1-2   Primary 1-6   JHS   No
                                                                 English

Q7.   Does your school run a phonics programme?

Yes   No

Q8.   Please can you specify the type of structure to your programme, if any?

Structured   Semi-structured   Randomly   Not
                                        Structured   Structured

Q9   Which **best** describes the phonics programme you run in your school?

Individual   Don't   whole words   Not

Letters   run a   broken up   sure

Sounded to   programme   then

form words   sounded

Q10. Which of the following do you think **best** describes a <u>synthetic</u> phonics programme?

Breaking	Semantics	Blending of	All
down parts	design	individual	
of whole words		phonemes	
to blend		to form words	

Q11. Which of the following do you think **best** describes an <u>analytic</u> phonics programme?

Breaking	Semantics	Blending of	All
down parts	design	individual	
of whole words		phonemes	
to blend		to form words	

Q12 Which programme would you adopt as the main approach to the teaching of phonics?

Synthetic	None	Analytic	Need more information

Q13 Finally, would you consider a structured phonics programme to assist the teaching of English in your school?

Yes	No

Thank- you for completing this questionnaire!!

www.ingramcontent.com/pod-product-compliance
Lightning Source LLC
Chambersburg PA
CBHW071256170526
45165CB00003B/1365